Turn Me On

By

Jody N. Holland

And

Mike Grigsby

DEDICATION

This book is dedicated to all the speakers out there who wish to build their connections, inspire their audiences, and turn on the excitement in those who come to hear them. Whether you are a manager, trainer, speaker, or top executive, our hope is that these words will light a fire in you and equip you to be the shining light your teams need.

CONTENTS

ACKNOWLEDGMENTS

I would like to thank my wife, Renae, for her editing and review of the book. I would like to thank the hundreds of companies who have repeatedly given me the opportunity to speak and present for them. I would like to thank the groups who have brought me in for their annual conferences, staff development and more, and let me "Turn Their Teams On" for success!

Jody N. Holland

I would like to acknowledge the speakers in my life who have inspired me to keep getting back up in front of groups and sharing my thoughts. I have been truly blessed to have the chance to "Turn On" audiences for the last couple of decades, and I'm looking forward to the next couple!

Mike Grigsby

FOREWORD

I remember the first time that I was on stage…well, maybe not the first time, but certainly the first memorable time that I was on stage. I kept remembering the "Brady Bunch" episode where Jan was told to think of the audience in their underwear to help her feel at ease. I tried doing this and ended up with a whole new set of problems! What finally settled me down was remembering that if I messed up, there was no-one in the audience who would know it if I just kept the show going. I don't remember when I learned that little nugget, but it has paid huge dividends for much of my adult life.

Making presentations is such a commonplace activity in life that you would be hard-pressed to find someone who has never made some kind of presentation. Whether delivering the State of the Union address, talking to a Girl Scout troop, making a sales pitch, or gossiping with a friend, all of us, at one time or another, have made some kind of presentation.

I have heard countless people state how terrified they are of public speaking – my wife being the most ardent! She has a dickens of a time getting in front of people but will engage an absolute stranger, one on one, about nearly anything under the sun. I have met people whose palms get sweaty, whose mouths dry up and who suffer mild to severe anxiety attacks, all at the notion of having to speak in front of a crowd.

If this is the camp you find yourself in, then this book was written with you in mind. If you're a seasoned presenter with nerves of steel standing before the masses, fear not, we haven't left you out. You'll find plenty of high-level tips and strategies that you can use to sharpen and hone your skills to kick your presentations up a notch.

Jody and I had a lot of fun writing this book. It was often side-splittingly hilarious as we revisited some of our most embarrassing moments as presenters, and we were literally amazed at the number of times we simply "winged it" and got the ovation of our lives. We hope that you enjoy the stories, devour the tips and strategies and make a sincere choice to step into

your A-game and become a presentation all-star.
Blessings! -- *Mike Grigsby*

Like Mike, I remember the early start that I had. My
father is a Methodist Minister and I used to go on
Saturdays to listen to him enthrall even the very pews
that people would be sitting in the next morning. I
loved how captivated I felt when I was in the
congregation. I loved listening to people on Sunday
mornings when they would shake his hand after the
service and tell him that they felt like he had spoken
only to them. The amazing thing to me was to hear
20% or more of the congregation say the same thing.
At the age of 4, I would organize my cousins into an
audience and deliver an address about the importance
of, well anything that I could think of. I remember
dressing in a military-style uniform. I loved the feel of
being in front of people.

What I learned in those early years is that people want
to see your speech more than they want to hear it.
They want to feel something in a world where we
have grown too numb.

I am not sure what it really feels like to be terrified of speaking in public. Because of the pushing from my father, I had lots of opportunities to overcome that fear before I was smart enough to know that I should be scared. Speaking, particularly when you are turning the audience on, and lighting their fire or jazzing them up, is an artistic exchange of energy and passion. Great speakers are as dependent on the audience as they are on their materials.

As Mike said, we have had a great time putting this together, remembering our journey toward growing into our stage presence, and mapping out the essence of what has allowed us to be invited to speak around the country and at times in foreign lands.

--Jody Holland

INTRODUCTION

He stood at the back of the stage, palms tingling slightly. He went through the mantra that had brought him luck in the past. He knew this was the big speech, the one that mattered to his ego. He was being recognized as a top salesperson in the distribution company that he worked with. He had been with them since Year One. He had bet his business partner that he, unlike any of the other speakers so far, would definitely receive a standing ovation. He would bring the audience to their feet and walk off the stage to resounding applause.

That he, was me, Jody Holland. I was the arrogant little twit (Mike's words, not mine) that had bet Mike that I could outshine every other speaker from the previous two days. My speech topic…the keys to successful selling. I had been told that I could have up to seven minutes for my acceptance speech and I was determined to take it all. I came up with the 5 key actions of a top salesperson.

Action 1: Know your products and how they can help your prospects to achieve their desired outcomes.

Action 2: Become a student of yourself. Know yourself and invest in your personal growth.

Action 3: Focus on helping, not selling. The focus had to always be on helping other people solve the challenges that kept them up at night.

Action 4: Operate inside of a system. Have a system for every step in the sales and service process. Don't wing it! That never works in the long-term.

Action 5: Drum roll please… (Note: At this point I asked everyone in the audience to stand up so that they could really grasp the intensity of the last and most profound action. They all stood up.) As the audience stood, I said "You just performed the most important action. You got off your butts. Now go sell something!"

At this point, the audience exploded into applause. And, Mike owed me $20. I had pulled off what others, including the president of the company, had not. I had turned the audience on. I used the techniques that I had mastered over 23 years of public speaking at that point in order to flip that switch and get them ready for a victory of their own. I had learned that a great speaker isn't the one with the most content. A great speaker is the one whose content means the most to the group. A great speaker is one who connects with the individual members of the audience, taps into their emotions, and gets them to see, feel and touch a vision of who they know they can be and who they really ought to be. As you go through this book, you will learn the techniques that will bring an audience to their feet, inspire your managers to walk through fire with you, and build a rapport with executives that gets them to ask the question of how they can buy from you. We will share with you the wisdom, humor, pain and success that we have had along the way and take your hand and walk you up to the precipice of speaking success.

My warning to you is this: We intend to challenge your philosophical perspectives and crush what your speech teacher taught you when you were but a pimple-faced youngster. We are not going to teach you how to put people to sleep. We are going to teach you how to wake up their souls, swell their hearts, and inspire them to take action. We are going to bring you along on the journey that we both began before we started school and will be on for the rest of our lives. So put on your sunglasses and get ready for the switch to flip! Let's turn that audience on!

JODY HOLLAND

1 GREAT PRESENTERS ARE BORN – SOMETIMES

The title of this chapter is an absolute! All great presenters are born. That isn't to say that they are born to be great presenters or that talent is even natural. It is simply that there is a birthing process that takes place in the evolution of presentation. They are born into greatness through practice, learning, participation, more learning, critique and guidance. They are born into greatness through a willingness to learn and adapt and a dismissal of the ego's need to be right all the time. Just like great athletes, it is the hard work and great coaching that gets you where you need to be. Michael Jordan was not born with a basketball in his hands.

J.K. Rowling went from being a divorced single mom who had no money and attended night school, to become one of the richest women in the world. Harry Potter's magic came from inside of her. Her stage is in the printed realm. She presented an enchanting story that drew in millions of people and made her one of the greatest writers known. Oprah Winfrey was once fired from her position as a TV personality because she was "unfit for TV." Mel Tillis, who has a sever stutter, went on to be an iconic singer and even a stand-up comedian. Had any of these people listened to what the world was telling them, they would be in positions that never capitalized on their true inner strength and never allowed them to succeed to the degree that they subsequently did.

Knowing who you can be and knowing what the world has told you about your presentations are two different things. David Letterman was made fun of in high school because of his big teeth and was laughed at when he told people he would one day be a famous TV personality. Each of us is born with the seeds of potential inside of us. We may not have been born with the natural talents of a public speaker, but very few people actually were. During your developmental years you were exposed to things that would have made speaking in public either easier or more difficult. You were not put into a position in which you could not succeed, though. That is simply a decision that you have to make.

As a presenter, you are starring in a role. The reason that people seem to struggle so much with being in front of a group is that they are amateurs. It is they, actually they, who are in front of the group. But you have to understand that it is your *presenter*, the pro inside of you, that is in front of the group. It isn't you as a person, but you as a *presenter*. Becoming a professional speaker requires you to be a speaker, not to be a person. Zig Ziglar understood that he was there to prime the pump on his audience and to get their motivational juices flowing. He was not there to have a conversation. He was there to create an internal conversation in your mind and in your heart. Creating this separation in your mind between what your stage presence is and what your everyday presence is will clear up the confusion of you thinking that YOU have to be the great presenter. It is YOUR presenter inside of you that goes to work when the time is right. So, the first critical component for you to understand is that you have to create your presenter, hire them to do their job, and then get out of their way.

Great presenters are not born that way! They are invented, created, employed! Invent the persona that you want. Create the characteristics of greatness by describing them in detail and comparing them to other greats that you look up to. Now, employ that person to the fullest capacity and watch the crowds engage at a truly deep level.

The second component of being a great presenter is the reality that talent is wasted on the gifted. This can seem to be a bit of a harsh statement to some, particularly those who are naturally talented in an area. The reason that talent is wasted on the gifted is that these are the people who often tend to show up and do what they are naturally gifted to do, but they do not put in the hours. They don't practice their gift the way that someone who has to work at it would practice. There is a three-step process that all great presenters follow to develop their skills and increase the positive reaction that they receive from the audience.

<u>Step 1</u>: Identify the characteristics that you wish to possess. This is done from modeling great presenters. Watch the physical characteristics of the person. Watch how they engage their audience. Listen to their style of speech. Listen to how they respond to the audience as they are speaking. Keep in mind that 93% of all listening is done non-verbally. This means that your facial expressions, tone of voice and gestures are what require the most attention. Speakers who are truly engaging do not stand still to deliver their message. Having great content is only a small part of being a great presenter. The much bigger part is giving the right delivery of that content.

Take notes on speakers. Go and see them live. Identify what evokes emotions in you. Ask the people around you what evokes emotions in them when they are listening to great speakers.

<u>Step 2</u>: Give as many speeches and presentations as you can, attempting each time to mimic what the greats are doing. This does not mean that you should be those people. Instead, you want to be you, with all of those great characteristics embodied in your

collective style. The tough part here is to videotape as many of these speeches as you can and then have people who will be brutally honest with you evaluate your effectiveness in embodying this new style.

Step 3: Give the same speech at least one dozen times, evaluating each time what is working and what is not working. Repetition creates familiarity and enables adaptations to be made with comfort and ease. Zig Ziglar indicated that he would practice his famous speech on "Priming The Pump" three or four times before each delivery of the speech. If someone who was considered a speaking legend was still practicing a speech that they had given more than one thousand times, what makes you think that you don't need to practice? The truth is that we do need to practice. People who are gifted at speaking impromptu often take for granted that the audience is responding. Imagine for a moment what kind of reaction you could achieve if you could deliver your presentation in such a way that you literally did not have to think. Not having to think means that the presentation is now a natural extension of who you are. In the development of a skill set, it takes approximately 2,500 repetitions of a skill to make it a natural extension of who you are. Keep in mind that the goal is to deliver 2,500 speeches in order to attain the title of Master Speaker. With every speech that you practice, you will notice that it becomes easier to remember the content and to add your nonverbal flare to its delivery.

To bring it all together, consider the idea that by practicing the right skill with the right evaluation, and mimicking the right desirable qualities, you are born into greatness as a speaker. This right repetition moves you through the continuum of skills development into a state in which the skill becomes part of who you are. If it is your objective to become one with the skill, then and only then will you be born into greatness as a speaker. Then and only then will your name become synonymous with being one of the greats in the world of speaking.

Find the speakers who you wish to emulate. Study their style of delivery. Record yourself, evaluate yourself, and get others to evaluate you as well. Keep in mind that you don't need people to stroke your ego here. Instead, you need people to be honest with you. And finally, never forget the old question about how you get to Carnegie Hall – you get there through PRACTICE, PRACTICE, PRACTICE!

Jody Holland

2 BE THE AUDIENCE –
WOULD YOU LISTEN TO YOURSELF?

One of the more difficult exercises that I have participated in is that of recording myself and then seeing if it held my attention. But putting myself in the audience and listening to myself as a presenter has helped me in a lot of ways. Just like watching a game film for a football player, studying fighters for the student of martial arts, or reviewing great movies for the actor, I needed to see me in action. Having gone through this process a number of times, there are some specific techniques and a step-by-step process that I would recommend you follow in order to get the best results in your personal development, to be able to turn an audience on instead of off.

1. 93% of all communication happens through non-verbal means. This means that *how* you say your speech is more important than what you say in it. When presenting to the boss, if you are nervous, it shows in your non-verbal

communication. If you are supremely confident about the direction that you are taking a presentation in, it shows without your words. I remember hearing a speaker talking about facial expressions and indicating that there are approximately 2,000 muscular combinations for the face. That is a lot of facial manipulation. I know that there are speakers who I can simply watch and never hear, but I can't look away. So, step one in your practice of becoming the person that you would absolutely love to hear is to be the person that you don't hear. Well, I don't want you to hear with your ears anyway. Your first challenge is to talk for a minimum of three minutes about a topic that is important to you, and record the whole thing. You have to record yourself speaking about this important topic and simply observe your presentation style. When you play it back, I want you to turn the sound off on the TV/computer/camera. Watch the way in which you move your hands and arms. Watch the way you form the words, the movement of your eyes, the emphasis that you imagine from simply observing the speech. Once you have watched it, I want you to go back and record the same topic again, but this time try to over-exaggerate the story with your body language and facial expressions. Imagine that you are an actor in the biggest theatrical production of your career. You are tasked with demonstrating too much nonverbal expression. Once you have recorded that, go back and review the tape again, this time looking for how it changes your perspective on the story. In all of your reviews, I want you to watch with no sound. This is important to get a full picture of whether or not you can captivate and turn the audience on, or if you look like you're taking a nap.

2. Tone of voice, pitch, and inflection are key components of giving a great presentation. You probably remember your lessons from early childhood when your mother told you not to talk to her in that tone of voice. You

were likely befuddled by the chastising, the same way I was the first few times. Your tone is the emotional appeal or connection that you have with the audience. Your tone should portray specific feelings at key points in your presentation. I would like for you to have a friend review the tapes that you have from your prior practice. I don't want them to watch them, though. I want them to simply listen to them and write down the emotions that they believe you intended to convey in the order that they recognize them. If the only emotion they get is boredom, that isn't good. We want them to hear your passion, your excitement, your fear, your joy, and so on. If they did not hear the emotions that you thought you were portraying, then you were likely not portraying those emotions in a way that people would connect with you. You want to go back and try a few more times to make sure that when people listen to you, they are connecting to the emotions that you intended for them to experience. You also want to ask for their feedback, as well as providing your own, on the inflection and pitch of your voice. Is your voice pleasing to listen to? Does it have enough variation from low to high to keep the audience paying attention? You never want to stay at one pitch for very long because the brains of the audience will quickly begin to shut down. They need to be "chasing your pitch" a little. There is a balance here. You don't want to come across as a 14-year old boy going through puberty. Rather, you want to have variations that make listening to you fun. Finally, they need to feel connected through your eyes. The eyes are the window to the soul, but they are also the link between one soul and another. The most simplistic explanation that I can add here is to pick one person on the left, one in the middle, and one on the right side of the room in which you are speaking. You want to jump around between those three people, making contact for a couple of seconds each time with each one of them. You really want to key in on people who are giving off signals of attentiveness. This would be people who are leaning forward a little, nodding their heads and giving signs that you are one incredibly entertaining speaker. This technique of audience scanning makes people feel that you are speaking directly to them and are connecting with them at a deep level.

3. Tell a story. I have never met anyone who did not like a good story. The key is to draw your audience into the story in such a way that they are experiencing the emotions you are portraying. All great stories contain a conflict. Whatever story you come up with to underline what your topic is has to have a good conflict. This draws people in and makes them want to cheer for the hero who finds resolution, rescues the damsel in distress, slays the dragon, marries his beloved, etc. You get the picture. Without a conflict, it is boring. If the story of "Twilight" did not have a conflict between Jacob and Edward,

with Bella in the middle, it would just be shiny people who kill mountain lions. In other words, that story would "bite." We love a good conflict. We love it almost as much as we love the hero winning out in the end. You need to be able to tie a story to your point in order to draw your audience in. Metaphors can accomplish that, as can real-life experiences. Those experiences don't even have to be yours. They can be stories from history that end in triumph. Remember, no-one writes books about people who end up losing or quitting. The stories that people want to hear are ones about overcoming adversity. Your story or the stories of others can inspire and engage at an incredibly deep level, particularly if you combine it with the effective use of all of the key aspects of nonverbal communication.

We only listen as long as the story is interesting. We only listen to people who are connecting with us. We only listen to people who have something important to say. Through practice and review, you can develop the skills of great nonverbal communication – the effective use of pitch, tone and inflection – and will ultimately tell one incredible story. At the end of the day, if you wouldn't want to listen to yourself all day long, change your style. It doesn't mean you should quit presenting. It means that you should quit presenting in that style.

Style and flare are what set the great presenters apart from the mediocre ones. Regardless of whether you are a speaker, supervisor, leader, or just wish to be an influencer, you have to practice putting your best face forward. Your presentation determines their receptiveness. You are in control and you can make this fantastic. If you are unsure of whether you are on the right path, you may want to consider having one of our Bold Culture coaches review some film of you. You can check out **boldculture.com** for more info on that.

3 ACT AS IF IDK IS A-OK

One of the great challenges that speakers face is the dissenter, the heckler, the trouble-maker, the person who just likes to disagree. It is this person who will ask questions to intentionally trip you up. They are the ones who will go out of their way to see if they can discredit you. The first thing you have to learn is that it is perfectly fine to not know every answer. You want to be as prepared as possible, but knowing everything is not currently possible.

The key is to handle the heckler in the right way. It is perfectly OK to say "I don't know the answer to that, but I will find out." I have found that people like learning from someone who is genuine. You are only genuine when you admit that you don't know everything. Your objective is, or at least should be, to connect with your audience. It doesn't matter if there are 10 people or 10,000 people in the audience, you have to develop a genuine connection.

So, how do you handle it? In my experience, you will need to be confident enough in yourself to tell the person who is questioning you that you have more to learn.

In my smaller groups (under 50), I will let people know that I have read dozens of books on giving presentations, hundreds on leadership, and even more on personal development. I then let people know that the more I learn, the more that I realize I need to learn. When you develop the right attitude related to your need to learn new things, you will be open to learn something from each person who considers themselves a student of you and your speaking.

It is your attitude that will set you up for success or failure when handling the tough people and the tough questions in your audience. You develop the right attitude by focusing on being a positive and happy person and by investing daily in learning something new. There are three keys to keeping your audience engaged when you don't know all the answers.

Key Number 1: Recognize each person in the group as

a valuable member of the group.

What I mean by this is that when you ask people to just wait or you say that you are not taking questions, people will begin to doubt you and will become turned off by the rest of what you have to share. You need to recognize the question from the person, clarify it if needed, and then proceed. If you know the answer, share it. If you are wanting to or are already planning on addressing that later, respond with...

"That is a great question!... In fact, it is so great that I already have that built into the presentation in just a bit. Would it be alright with you if I address it in the order that I have it in the presentation?" You want to use a warm and open expression when you say this. You want to be very careful not to use sarcasm or condescension in the way you present the message back.

If you don't know the answer and don't have any intention of addressing it later in the presentation, you should respond with something like...
"That is a great question. I want to make sure that I

give you the right answer. I am not sure what the right answer is right now, but I can find that out. Would you be willing to connect with me after the presentation so I can make sure I get your contact information? I want to make sure and get you the right answer." You will want to be very open and warm in your expression. You will even want to come across as appreciative.

You are not trying to get people to simply be quiet and listen. You are trying to let your audience know that you appreciate all of them, even the tough ones.

I want to share a story with you from my own life and personal experience. It was a Thursday and it was the fifth month of training that I had conducted for this organization. We had a contract to conduct 12 days of training with roughly 30 people in each of the sessions. I could tell without any doubt that one of the people in the group was unhappy to be there. He was unhappy because he was the training director for the organization and he had made it clear to his boss, who shared it with me, that he felt he was infinitely more qualified to develop and teach these programs than I was. He had refused to participate in discussions and wore a scowl on his face the entire time he was there. We were engaging in a discussion about how to effectively resolve conflict. Keep in mind that this gentleman had not said anything in the four previous classes. Right in the middle of the discussion, he unloaded his emotional baggage on me and his coworkers, indicating how angry he was that he had to be in these classes. After he finished his verbal tirade and the room was finally quiet, I looked at him and said, "That's awesome! I am so happy that you contributed!" The entire room broke out in laughter, including the person who had just cussed me out in front of the class. The tension was broken. More importantly, I did not allow his opinion to define me as a speaker. I smiled and made it clear that I was delighted that he had participated. For the rest of that class and for the next seven classes of that year of training, he participated. At the end of all 12 classes, he came up to me and thanked me. He appreciated the fact that he felt welcomed, even when he was not nice. He told me that he really did learn a lot and the classes had helped him.

<u>*Key Number 2*</u> is to genuinely believe that others have something to teach you.

The truth is that each person will approach learning from their own perspective. There is no one reality. There are, in fact, five billion plus interpretations of reality. The more perspectives that you can garner, the more equipped you will be to succeed as a presenter. This means that you have to see the value in each person whom you encounter. You have to look at people and genuinely love them for who they are, just as they are.

An example was when I was teaching a class for just over 100 people. These were people who were told to participate and told it was mandatory. They all felt that they were too busy to take time out to learn about leading. This sets a speaker up for a challenging audience. I had just quoted the "Law of the Lid" from John Maxwell's book *"The 21 Irrefutable Laws of Leadership,"* when a person stood up and said they couldn't stand the authors that I was quoting. At that time, I was quoting authors who were in the top ten of all leadership thinkers and writers. It caught me off guard because it was the first time I ever had someone complain about my ability to quote important ideas from multiple books. I stopped and looked at the woman who was now garnering massive attention from the rest of the group. I simply said, "There are thousands of writers on the subject of leadership; who is your favorite?" She was definitely caught off guard by my willingness to ask her this question. She responded that she liked Kouzes much better. I responded that I loved the book *"The Leadership Challenge."* Is that the book that she preferred? She slowly sat back down and said, "I think that is the one." She then continued, "I just get tired of people quoting the most popular authors. I wish there was more variety." I then responded with, "I am very open to other authors and would love to discuss authors with you after the program. Would you be willing to connect with me after the class so I can get some ideas from you on who to use to keep my quotations interesting?" She agreed and actually became engaged for the rest of the presentation.

This only worked because I truly care about people. I wake up in the mornings and look forward to being around people and learning from them. Adopt the attitude of gratitude in learning and people will respond positively.

Key Number 3 is to connect with the influencers.

I am a student of life. I am an observationalist (not a real word, but I am using it anyway). I love to see what others are doing and how they are doing it. I also love to see who the centers of influence are in every group. When you are dealing with groups of under 500, you can simply observe the crowd before your presentation and see who people naturally flock to. This is the person whom others want to get the approval of and be connected with. In some cases, it is simply the person whom others are afraid of.

John Wesley, who started the United Methodist Church, recounted stories of how he would ensure that the centers of influence were on his side. His preaching was done mostly near mines and on hillsides and various other places where those who needed religion the most would be. He was even known to preach inside taverns. In his particular case, he was not a man of tremendous physical stature. He was small. He would enter a tavern or a group of people where he wished to preach. He would spot the largest person there and would make his way to that person. He would introduce himself and ask if he could ask the gentleman a few questions. The person seemed to always be willing to answer questions. He would ask if he had ever done anything to offend the person. The person would answer "no" because they had never met him before. He would ask if he had ever wronged them in any way? They would again say "no". He would indicate that he wished to share some information with the group but found it most helpful to ensure that he was in good standing with the people he considered to be influencers. The large man he was talking to would assure him that he was in good standing. He would then say that since he did not know any of the people there, it would be great if his new friend would help him out and remind people, if necessary, that he had done nothing to offend anyone and simply wished to share some good news.

The large fellow would oblige, and John Wesley would commence his preaching. The same basic process works with any crowd that you are in. Your objective is to establish a connection with the influencers for the purpose of keeping things on track as you speak. It is ideal to have an influencer in the middle, on the left, and on the right. If you have not met anyone before you go on stage, then simply pick a person who is responding positively to you in each of those zones. By focusing on the person who is focusing on you, both of you will benefit. This will also help you to remember to scan the room from left to right and back. Your eye contact connection will be powerful and will really build the perceived connection with the audience.

Remembering and practicing these three keys will keep you on the path to success and will truly keep your audience "Turned On."

4 A NEW TWIST ON AN OLD REALITY

William James, considered the father of American psychology, said, "That which I perceive is my reality." Each of us will perceive truths in our own unique way. We will interpret things based on our collection of experiences. Oftentimes, our explanation of an old truth will unlock a new reality for someone else. It is this phenomenon that makes hearing a great presenter so engaging, fun and even enlightening.

Your ability to simplify the complex creates a learning opportunity for everyone who experiences your speaking. People who try to complicate the simple and make the complex impossible are the speakers who simply frustrate the masses and cater to those who consider themselves intellectual elites. Your primary objective as a speaker should be to make each thing that you discuss more understandable, more clear, and more attainable.

Zig Zglar was a master communicator who could take

old ideas and rejuvenate them in such a way that all of us could understand them. He related to everyone and could connect with anyone. He could draw out the knowledge that you have in your psyche by relating to you and helping you "get it." What you are dealing with in speaking is a mass of realities that must be melded together to form a new reality that makes something inspiring.

The saying "There is nothing new under the sun" explains the truth that we are simply adding to, taking away from, or reshaping ideas that have been in existence since the beginning. We put our twist on the ideas in order to make them more easily understood by others. An example of this would be the idea of manifesting your goals. In the book, *"The Secret,"* the authors talk about using the power of intention to make your goals come true for you. Napoleon Hill talked about the power of a definite purpose in his book, "Think And Grow Rich." This is essentially the same thing. Andrew Carnegie told Napoleon Hill about his concept of purpose that had built the steel empire that Carnegie had at the time. I am quite sure that Carnegie learned the lesson from someone else. All the way back through recorded history, you see examples of this and see that it is NOT a new concept.

The truths that we impart go back hundreds, even thousands of years. They may even go back farther than any recorded history that we have. We are not inventing new concepts. We are simply sharing our version of the concept. You are at your most authentic, and most believable, when you present from who you are. If you are simply presenting what someone else believes, it comes out in your presentation. People can tell when you are being genuine. You must take the time to form your own opinions and stop being afraid of other people not agreeing with you. The reason that you get hired, over someone just reading a book, is that you present the information in a way that other people have not seen or heard before. They come to see how you put a twist on the reality that they live in. They are seeking that new perspective.

My recommendation is that you pull from the old

bridal tradition of "Something old, something new, something borrowed, something blue." It is the multiplicity of perspectives that helps people shape their own opinions effectively in their own minds. Look at the origins of words and phrases to bring about the "something old" portion of your presentation. The website **etymonline.com** is a great place to start. Learning the origins of words is a fantastic way to start any presentation. You impress people when you know where something came from, or how it got started.

The New Dictionary of Cultural Literacy is another great resource. You can buy it on **amazon.com** for about $20. This book helps you understand the origins of phrases and sayings. It is a fantastic reference book for quotations and allows you to expand your capacity to explain what the original meaning of things was and what the meanings have evolved into. The internet itself is also a great resource when it comes to learning where things came from and how they have evolved.

When looking for something new to include in your speeches, you will want to be up to speed on current books and current ideas from thought leaders. In the next chapter, we will talk about the fact that leaders are readers.

One of the best pieces of advice I have ever received was the admonition to read at least one new book per month for personal development. By exposing yourself continuously to new ideas, you will always have a new twist on an old idea to talk about. You add credibility to your presentation by being "up" on the newest concepts. If you don't read new books, you will find that it is difficult to relate to the people in your audience. Knowing what current leaders are saying and writing will position you to be one of them. Read, learn and persuade in your presentations.

When identifying the things that you wish to borrow, look to the concepts that have already been blended together relating to your topic. One of the key ways to accomplish this is to see what concepts have already been rehashed. If you have done your homework on the origins of words and phrases, you will be better prepared to make the correlations of one concept to the next iteration of that concept. Your topic or concept will always make the most sense when it is explained in a variety of ways. It is the variation of thought that helps others to borrow your concept and make it their own. Ultimately, you will borrow concepts and put your own twist on those concepts. By making them uniquely yours, you will set yourself up for helping people to see the possibilities of the future.

Something blue, or something that prompts blue sky dreaming, can be created by getting people to visualize the possibilities. It is in dreaming that we are most awake. A strong part of your objective in giving a great presentation is to get others to see the possibilities that exist for them. That blue sky – the unbridled possibilities – represents the concepts that move people to action. Great presentations always call for people to do something differently than they have done before. This requires people to open their minds to ideas of what could be possible if they were willing to do something differently. You must build the blue-sky concepts into your presentation. The human mind thinks in the present tense and in pictures. This means that in order to achieve the blue-sky effect you will have to prime your audience to see their future now and to see a picture of how great it really is. This is often accomplished by saying something to the effect of...

"Today is [insert one year from today]. You wake up first thing this morning and you realize that you have taken consistent action over the past year. You see your new car in the driveway. You see the two books you have written on the shelf, one of which has the tag "New York Times Best Seller" on the front cover. You realize that all your actions have led you to this moment. You are a success because you have acted just like a success for the last year. You are a winner!"

It is this visualization in the present tense that sets you apart from the rest of the crowd of speakers. Once you master this concept, you will see people move themselves towards action at the end of your presentations. You will see the difference that it makes.

Your reality is the truth created from the truths that have existed in the past. Your concepts will make the most sense to your audiences when they are supported by concepts that have existed for years. Don't be afraid to create something that is uniquely yours yet still blended from things that have existed for decades or even centuries. You have something amazing to offer others. This offering is the wisdom you can pull together from what others have presented in the past. So, go and create something old, something new, something borrowed and something blue!

5 LOOK, LISTEN AND LEARN

There's an opportunity to learn in every experience, and every experience can be grafted into your presentations. I've always said that real genius is the ability to find the connection between two disparate points. Steve Jobs found a way to connect calligraphy and computers. Hall of Fame wide receiver Lynn Swann found a way to connect ballet with football. Jesus brought the Divine down to earth through parables. Elaborating on one point through a simple illustration of something completely disconnected is often one of the best tools for cementing an idea with your audience.

If you want to lead, begin to read.

You already know what you know, now it's time to begin to learn what other people know. Spend time reading. Read everything from newspaper articles to trade journals, to technical manuals, to novels, to comic books. This helps you to not only exercise your own skills – like going to the gym for a workout – but it helps keep your mind flexible and your arsenal fully stocked. I cannot tell you how many times I have read a blog, an article or the back of a cereal box and found something that I later used in a presentation. This kind of well-roundedness gives your presentations depth and personality and brings a relevance that would not otherwise be there...

One of the critical factors of your success as a speaker or presenter will be your ability to have something new to offer. This could be a new spin on an old concept, a new concept that makes life easier, or even a new attitude that people can take with them. Learning new things is as easy as L-1, L-2, L-3. You have to be <u>looking</u> for things to learn. You have to be <u>listening</u> to what others have to teach. And you have to be <u>learning</u> from every experience. Let's dive into those three aspects of how you enhance the material that you have to offer your audiences.

LOOK.

Looking for things to learn starts with the belief that

there is something else that you need to know. In the beginning of this chapter, we said that you already know what you know. The challenge that many of us have is that we don't know what we don't know. The even bigger challenge is that we are doing our best to NOT figure out what those things are. The day that you believe that you know everything that you need to know is the day that you stop learning altogether. John Lubbock said, "You get what you are looking for." To me that means that we will never have a new experience, a new tidbit of knowledge, or a new idea if we aren't looking for them. I remember a story that my father used to tell when I was young. I have paraphrased it below.

A man was digging around in the grass below a street lamp, obviously looking for something of value. I watched him for a minute to see what all of his crawling around was about. Then I approached the man and asked if I could help. He looked up at me with an expression that denoted both panic and gratitude and said, "Sir, I would really appreciate that. I've lost my keys and have to find them in order to get home to my family." Me, being the kind of person who understands how great family life is and how you long for them when you are away from them, knew that this was important. I sat my bag down and began looking through the grass as well. At first, I stayed up on my feet, but eventually decided that I could only be truly effective if I got down on my knees and crawled around in the grass as well. We searched and searched for 15 minutes. Finally, in frustration myself, I asked him "do you remember exactly where you lost them?" He looked at me, slightly dismayed by the question and answered "yes." He said, "I lost them about 20 feet in that direction" and he pointed away from the light. "But the light is just so much better over here."

How many times do people try to take the easy way and look for things where they will never find them? How many times have you known where to look for the answers, but still decided to look someplace else? I have heard CEOs, executives and even college presidents give presentations that were horrible. They were boring, told bad stories, irritated people and then walked around looking for praise. It was obvious to everyone but the presenter that the presentation was bad. In this case they were not looking for ways to get better. They were looking for affirmation that they were okay. Look for feedback on your presentations. Look for lessons that can be learned every day in life. Look for opportunities to grow and develop. Most importantly, look inside of yourself and discover whether or not you believe you still have more to learn. If you don't believe you have more to learn, you won't learn anything new. Your beliefs will lead to your attitude, which will lead to your thoughts, which will lead to your behaviors, which will lead to your results. If you want better results, look for things you can change in yourself in order to get those results.

I am a big believer in organizations that want to help you grow as a presenter. Toastmasters,® the National Speakers Association (NSA), as well as others, all have the purpose of helping you become the best version of you possible. They will critique you, evaluate you and help you become better. You have to look for a group in your area, though. I would encourage you, especially if you are new to the presentation game, to begin with Toastmasters.® Do you believe that you should look in the right place for personal growth or are you simply going to look where the light is better and hope to accidentally experience a miracle in personal growth?

LISTEN.

The second aspect of success is to listen to what is being said. This applies to both the feedback that you get from your peers as well as what you are able to observe in life. I love watching movies. I love the creativity that went into making the movie and I love the escape into someone else's imagination. I love to listen to what their mind has to say. I get lessons regularly from movies that I can use in my presentations.

Not only do I get lessons from movies, I get them from the mall, from my kids, from airports, from random strangers, and more. If you believe that you have lots to learn, then you will listen to all that there is to learn in this world. If you don't believe you have more to learn, then you won't listen to what the world has to offer.

I would encourage you to take a notebook (paper or electronic) with you everywhere you go. You never know when an idea will occur for a speech or a lesson that you can share. Listening means that you are observing others, searching for something great from what they say or do, and internalizing what you can learn from them.

Listening is a contact sport. It involves getting in the middle of someone else's ideas without pushing your ideas on them. You have to see others as wonderful creations that offer insight and opportunity. Even the most difficult person has something to offer. When you listen, you have to use your eyes to observe the physical lessons that are there to learn. You have to use your ears to hear the audible lessons that life has to offer. You have to use your emotions/feelings to experience the underlying intent of the lesson.

When you immerse yourself in the experiences that you have been looking for, you will engage all facets of your listening. This sets you up for the third key, which is to learn the lessons that are offered to you.

LEARN.

We only learn what we are open to learn. This simple statement pretty well sums up why so many people in this world continue to make the same mistakes over and over again. In my discussions with larger companies in the United States, I began to ask a question about their mistakes. I began asking, "How many mistakes that happened this year have happened before?" The amusing and sad answer that I keep getting is "all of them." This would mean that people are making the same mistakes that they made before. This also means that people are NOT learning from their past mistakes. A short parable that I believe illustrates this point is....

My uncle was a very successful banker. He made great loans to people who would pay them back and he consistently earned a profit for the bank that employed him. As a bank president, he had seen all kinds of loan officers over the years. This one young gentleman, we'll call him Hank, mostly because that was his name, was more eager than most to be successful. I remember the conversation that Hank and my uncle had on a Monday morning as I sat in the corner of the office. "Mr. Schaef, I really want to be as successful as you are. I have been very impressed with how well you are able to read people and the consistency of your success. I have every intention of being as successful as you are." "That's fantastic, Hank. I want you to be that successful." "Me too sir, but I had a question. What is the secret to your success?"

"That's easy, Hank! I only loan money to people who are going to pay it back. As long as you don't make mistakes on that, everything will be great!"

Slightly befuddled, Hank looked at my uncle and asked, "But how do you keep from making mistakes?"

"Well, if you follow the path I took, you first loan money to people who won't pay it back and make some bad mistakes. You then get chewed out by your boss for making mistakes and you sit and listen to the things that he says. Then, you apply the wisdom he shared with you and become successful like me."

Hank thought about that for a minute and asked, "Isn't

there an easier way?"

"Sure," my uncle replied. "You could take the time to learn from the mistakes of others instead of insisting on making them all yourself. In hindsight, I really wish I would have taken that path."

We will all make mistakes. We don't have to make all of them, though. I believe that intelligence is learning from your mistakes. I believe that wisdom is learning from the mistakes of others. My question to you is, are you seeking wisdom in your life? If you are, you will learn from what others have to offer. Every presentation that you see will teach you something. Every training session you attend will leave you with a little more to offer the world. If you are seeking only intelligence, you will have to make all of your mistakes yourself and experience the pain of defeat in order to believe the lesson.

6 PLAGIARIZE NICELY

Death by Bullet Point

You gotta stop reading the slides! The slides are there for your audience, not you. Look, just because you *can* fit your entire presentation on your slide in a 4pt font, doesn't mean you *should*. Your slides are there to summarize – into brief statements – the fuller content of what you are saying. If you are relying on the slideshow to be your presentation, shame on you. This reveals a complete lack of preparation, a lethargy in engaging the audience and a complete refusal to learn your material.

The simple truth about presenting is that you have to be fun enough to look at and listen to so that people walk away thinking about wanting to see you and listen to you again. Time and time again, I hear people complain about presenters who feel that the slides are why they are in the room. It is sad to me to think about the number of companies that pay for training each year so that their leaders or sales people or whomever can have a good nap. If the trainer is not "edu-taining" the participants, then the participants are not learning anything. One of the most important things I have ever done is learn to model the great speakers out there. This means that I had to unlearn most of what I learned in college about speaking in public. I had to learn to move like a jungle cat, keeping my audience enthralled with the idea that my next point was about to pounce on their brain. I had to educate them with the information that I just knew, not the information that I just read. Just as importantly, I had to entertain them with the way that I presented the information. Your presentation should be just as good without PowerPoint as it is with PowerPoint.

Most of the presentations that we develop will have a picture on the screen that relates to the subject we are talking about on that slide. Sometimes, they will have a quote. We need to keep it simple, though. If we complicate it, people will stop listening and start reading. And that is only half of it.

At least five times per year, none of the technology works where I am speaking. I present between 120 and 200 days per year. Five out of 120 isn't really that bad from a percentages standpoint. However, even one presentation in which I have no idea what to say – because I can't read the screen – means I am not really a presenter. People don't hire superstars just to read to them. They hire superstars to *present* to them. Make sure you aren't planning on the computer being the central theme of your presence. Make it about edu-taining your audience with your cat-like movement, your royal wit and unyielding charm. Then and only then will you be able to avoid the frustration of tech not working.

Sun spots, solar flares and swamp gas.

I have yet to make a presentation where I have not experienced some level of technical difficulty. The computer, the sound, the slide clicker, even the HVAC have all sought to sink my well-planned delivery. Long before the advent of Power Point™

and all of the technology we've come to rely on today, I was always in the habit of checking the carousel holding my 35mm slides before I started my presentation; one of them invariably would be reversed or flipped upside down. Sometimes there's just no reason why things go wrong. Chalk it up to sun spots, solar flares or swamp gas, but no matter the cause, you gotta have a backup plan! You've got to learn to roll with it and seamlessly transition to your contingency plan, because you can't outrun the long arm of Murphy's law!

I would argue that there is some cosmic training god out there who simply wants to test your capacity for recovery. I have had my laptop die in the middle of a presentation when I had left my notes at home. I have had the projector bulb burn out. I have done presentations where people fell over backwards in their chair because they leaned too far. I have had my voice start to disappear the night before a healthcare presentation to 2,000 doctors and nurses. I have been asked ten minutes before my 60-minute presentation to stretch it to three hours because the other two presenters didn't show up. I have even had the power go completely out in the entire building. The point is... I have to know my stuff inside and out, forwards and backwards, in short and long versions, with or without technology.

Like Mike, I spend an inordinate amount of time preparing for the presentation. I practice it in the mirror. I even record my presentations and then critique my movements. I then re-record the presentation with my new physical presence. All of this is critical to my success and will be critical to your success as well. I may not be able to outrun the long arm of Murphy's law, but I can dang sure beat the crap out of Murphy when he shows up. I do that by being prepared for everything I can think of and a few things that I never would have thought of. The more simplistic you keep the presentation, the more likely you are to nail the technological aspect of it.

The other side of this reality is that you need to know how to use technology. If something breaks, don't think that the pimple-faced 19-year old who is the "technology consultant" for the convention center is going to have an actual clue about what to do. I have had at least 50 different opportunities to fix problems for other speakers who either followed or preceded me at conferences. These are people who are "expert" presenters (*insert big cough and the letters B.S. here*) and they stored their presentation on a "stick thingy" [external hard drive]. They did not bring a backup laptop, nor did they have their presentation saved in multiple formats in case the provided laptop was different than theirs. Know about computers. Know about projectors. Know about audio equipment. Know about file formats and thumb drives (not stick thingies). If you are a professional presenter, you need to know about more than just the material you are presenting. You need to know how to make the presentation work. If you are unsure of how to operate any of this equipment, then go to Best Buy and start asking questions. Get on YouTube and search for how-to videos on the subject. There is plenty of information out there on how it all works. You simply have to take the initiative to learn it.

Technical difficulties come in the form of computer

problems, lighting and sound outages, wrong handouts, even people who don't know how to operate a chair. If you are focused on being the smartest person in the room instead of focused on imparting wisdom in a fun and witty style, you will succumb to Murphy's Law. If your objective is to entertain and educate, then your audience will love you with or without the bright shiny objects that technology provides. Take control of the presentation and be center stage in making it truly great! Remember, there is only one way to get to Carnegie Hall: Practice, practice, practice!

7 BEFORE THE CURTAIN GOES UP

The Whole World's A Stage

I have never understood why there is such a negative connotation to a presenter saying they must "turn it on" before a presentation. As if to say, if you don't have it "turned on" 24/7, then it's not real or sincere or genuine. Take a look at some of today's best screen and stage actors and they will tell you that they too have to "turn it on" before each performance. Oscar winner Henry Fonda was still throwing up before every stage performance, even when he was seventy-five!

It's one thing to be an expert in a given industry or field. It's something entirely different to be in front of people sharing your expertise. You must look at this as a performance, one that you must prepare for and be fully engaged in, whether you're delivering corporate training, making a sales pitch, or collecting a signature as a parcel delivery driver.

Most great speakers have a way to anchor their inner

presenter before going onstage. It is generally a ritual that they use to invoke the speaking deity that resides in their psyche. How you get that giant activated will depend on what works for you. There are some specific techniques that I have found to be incredibly helpful for me. I can only speak from my own experience. However, I have given more than 10,000 presentations and counting. I will walk you through what I do that gets me jazzed, psyched or pumped (insert your word here). I have my activation broken down into three steps.

1. The activation;
2. The inspiration;
3. The unleashing.

The *activation* is the first step. I have learned that the thought of staying turned on 100% of the time is exhausting in and of itself. Approximately 15 minutes before a presentation, I will close my eyes and take four deep breaths. I breathe in and hold it for a few seconds, and then exhale. I do this four times, all the while imagining that I am in a completely white room with no floor or ceiling or walls or anything else visible. In my mind, this is a place of pure potential. There is literally nothing there except for me, dressed in my presentation clothes. I allow the warmth of the room to wrap around me and comfort me for a minute or so. I then feel the light growing from the center of my chest. It is a ball of light and it grows and grows until it is larger than I am. As the light grows, all of the information I could possibly need for the presentation is awakened in my mind. I feel the electricity of thought pulsing through my head and the tingling of speaker perfection pulsating through every fiber of my body. I spend a couple of minutes simply thinking about how every great speaker that came before me was simply paving the way for me to dazzle the crowd I am about to step in front of.

The second step is the *inspiration*. At this point, my entire body is getting stoked about the opportunity I have been given to step in front of the crowd. The size of the crowd is irrelevant. I always bring the best of what I have to offer. I begin seeing the crowd assembled around me as an open possibility. I visualize the faces of the people being fully engaged in what I have to say. They are into everything I have to say and they hang on every word I say. I see myself giving the presentation and moving with such power that I can't even take my eyes off of me. It is like watching a movie that everyone is completely into. I see the presentation happening. I don't necessarily hear it happening. I just visualize it. I see myself going onstage, presenting, and concluding. I visualize the audience clapping loudly at the end of my presentation. I see people coming up to me and wanting my autograph. I see people leaving the location and calling their friends and family to share what they have learned from me and talking about how much they loved the presentation. I see their lives becoming better, their relationships improving, even the level of energy that they approach life with heightens. I spend a few minutes thinking about how much I want the audience to benefit from the information and how I wish only the best for them. I focus on amplifying the intensity of my desire to make their lives better for a couple of minutes. Then I am ready to unleash the speaking god.

The third step that I follow is to *unleash the speaker* that I have seen in my vision. To do this, I open my eyes and take a deep breath. I inhale success and exhale any fear or doubt. I inhale again and merge the vision of that perfect speaker with every fiber of who I am. I breathe in and tell myself that I have so much to offer this crowd and that I am going to make sure they walk away with strategies that will make their lives better. I breathe in and hold the breath for a few seconds. I then flex every muscle in my body and let out a yell in my mind. I activate the speaking warrior inside me by hearing his battle cry and watching as he runs in front of me. He is running into the battle and victory is mine by the time my foot hits the stage. And with that, I unleash THE SPEAKER and I am ready to turn my audience on.

8 MAY I HAVE ANOTHER HELPING, PLEASE?
Don't Forget the Burp!

In China and several other cultures outside of the United States, belching after dinner is the mark of a great meal and considered a high compliment. You want to leave your audience pining for more. Don't be afraid to pour yourself into each and every presentation, because no matter how much you give, the subliminal message is always, "There's more where that came from." End your time with your audience on a confident and positive note (regardless of subject matter) and let them know you'll be available afterward to take comments or answer questions. This is your second contact with your audience and where most follow-up requests come from....

The mark of a great presenter is the fact that people want to hire him/her again. I can clearly remember the first time a company asked me to come back and give the same speech again. My first thought was,

"Did I not cover the material well enough?" That wasn't it at all, though. They simply had so much fun with the presentation that they wanted a second helping. In 2000, at the turn of the century, I learned that people love hearing the same thing more than once when they get the right emotional stimulation from the presentation. It is the emotional appeal, not the logic of the material, that gets you an opportunity to come back.

The speeches I have given that people ask for over and over again are the ones that the audience walks away from with giant smiles on their faces, action-oriented thoughts on their minds and discussions about the topic filling the air around. My job is to unlock their motivation to go and do something great with their lives. Whether I am speaking on the generations, or leadership, or defining your purpose, or talent management, I strive to motivate people to go and DO something different than they were doing before. If I can launch change in people, they will want more of it.

There are three keys to being asked back as a speaker.

These keys are so logical and easy to understand, yet they are seldom actually implemented by speakers. In my mind, it actually defies logic to ever not do these three things:

1. *Knock their socks off!* Make sure you move like a jungle-cat, inspire the crowd like Gandhi, and share the wisdom of a guru. Give them all of who you are and do everything in your power to ensure they are dazzled into a near-hypnotic state of admiration. When you put all your energy and intelligence and capability into your presentation, people are impressed. If you don't do a great job, the other two components of this process aren't really that important. If you did your very best and delivered significantly more than anyone in the crowd expected, you can consider them sockless and happy.

2. *Plant the idea of asking you back in the minds of the listeners.* I don't mean that you have to throw dirt on them and sow speaking seeds into that dirt. I do, however, mean that you need to

have between three and five different points in your presentation in which you bring up the fact that you have more to present. You should bring up topics in your presentation and reference the fact that you have some great, in-depth information on that particular topic that you don't have time to sufficiently cover. You reference the fact that if they ask you back, you would love to share that in the first two references. In your third and subsequent references to the additional material, you refer to the fact that "when" they bring you back, you "will" cover that material. You are moving the group from thinking "this guy is great" to thinking "we should consider bringing him back," and finally to "I can't wait until we bring him back."

3. This is the truly unscientific one. This is the one that will make you pop yourself on the forehead and say, "Why didn't I think of that?" I end my presentations with this statement: "I have really enjoyed being with

you guys today. I can't wait to be with you again. I have a favor to ask of you. If you enjoyed the material today and you learned something, please go tell that to everyone that you have ever met. Post it on Facebook. Tweet it to your followers. Rent billboards to let others know how awesome it was. The billboards may be excessive but I am still okay with it. And if you didn't like it, please remember the lesson that I learned from my kindergarten teacher: nobody likes a whiner." I smile the biggest smile that I can and wave to the group or take a bow or simply tell them to make the rest of the day or week or year awesome.

Those three steps are not rocket science. But they have consistently gotten me invited back to do more, speak more, and bill more. If your desire is to be an incredible presenter, to make money by sharing wisdom, to dazzle crowds and engage audiences, then we are kindred spirits. We are on the same journey and we can help each other to achieve that destination. I can't wait to meet you at one of our live events. I can't wait to hear about how you have implemented these strategies and increased your billing, your influence, and your vigor in life. I want only the best for you and I want only success for you. So, until we have the opportunity to meet in person, I will leave you with this thought…

You are exactly where you have chosen to be in life. Every choice you have made has led you to this exact spot. I am truly excited about the choices that you will make from this point forward because your canvas is blank. You can paint the perfect future for yourself by equipping yourself with the skills of greatness and the attitude for achievement. When we see each other, I will high five your success and applaud your choice to be the winner that you were born to be. You were meant to "Turn On" audiences in your given area.

9 WHAT HAVE WE LEARNED?

The quality of the learning and interaction that occurs in a given setting are a direct reflection of the quality of our ability to present. Our job as presenters is to engage others to want to take action, to want to study, to want to be better. Essentially, our job is to uncover the motivational triggers that exist in each person in the room. If you have mastered the skills taught in this book, you will do just that. You will unlock each person's perceived potential in the subject area you are teaching. You will get them to see the possibility of what they can be, do and have. Great presenters understand this. They understand that it is about the audience and not about them. It is about reading and adjusting to the crowd in front of you, regardless of its size. It is about being the "YOU" that pushes the limits of their own self perception and raises their standards.

So, in order to make all this stick for you, let's review the eight key lessons that you have learned in this book and outline what you can do to continue learning.

1. **Great presenters are born.** Sometimes. Great presenters are born, literally, but they are not born as great presenters. Just like Michael Jordan became truly passionate about basketball and devoted almost all of his available time to mastering it, great presenters are passionate about their trade.

   The key difference between an amateur presenter and a professional presenter is that the pro HAD to find a way to do this for a living, because it was such an integral part of themselves.

   There are thousands of people in this world who say, "I really wish I could present like you" when they hear a great presenter. That isn't true, though. If they truly wished to be a great presenter, they would have already started working on it and it would have become their burning desire. Great presenters "go pro," while o.k. presenters work on giving a few speeches. Wake up every morning and "go pro" in a way that grabs opportunities to present.

2. **Be The Audience.** Stand in front of a full-length mirror, or record yourself with a video camera when you present. Do this without any other audience involved. You need to see how you move and how you engage yourself. If you don't look interesting to yourself, change your approach.

Watch the way in which great presenters move. It is their nonverbal actions that are engaging the audience, not just their words. When you uncover the reality that it is how you present more than what you present that will get you invited back, then you are on the right track. We would even encourage you to get a friend who can come listen to you a few times to see what works and what doesn't work.

3. **Act as if IDK is A-OK.** There are often groups in which you have a person whose favorite thing to do is disagree with you. If you let them get under your skin, you will lose the entire group. In order to beat the dissenter and engage the entire group, follow these three keys...

    a. *Value every member of the group as important.* Your belief about other people will always come out in the way you present. If you don't start with a foundation of believing – not just thinking, but believing that every member of the group is important and should be there – then you will not connect deeply. In fact, you will often come across as arrogant or uncaring. Every member of the group is important, they are just not all like you.

    b. *Believe that every member has something they can teach you.* Every person has something to offer. In the book

"Breakthrough Leadership" that Chip Townsend and Jody Holland co-authored, they talk about the need to be teachable at every level of success. When we are teachable, others are more naturally teachable as well. Set the pace for others to learn by being willing to learn from them first.

c. *Connect with the influencers.* There is always a key influencer in the group. When you can identify who that key influencer is quickly and get them on your side, the rest of the group tends to be much more cooperative. All you need is for the right person to say that they really want to hear what you have to say, and the others generally will follow along. John Wesley was a master at this. He quickly identified the key influencer in a group, connected with them and gained their trust, then they became a catalyst for others to engage in the presentation.

4. **A new twist on an old reality.** Your job is to make things easier to understand for the audience. Your job is to bring your reality, your understanding and your interpretation to the group. When you are good at synthesizing information, you find that others desire to hear what you have to say. People spend a great deal of time trying to come up with something that nobody has ever heard of before. The reality of life is that people need to understand what to do with what they have and with their current concepts first. They need to be able to grasp this new twist that you are able to bring to them. Make it easy. Make it simple. Make it fun.

5. **If you want to lead, you have to read.** Leaders in presenting understand how important it is to enhance their knowledge. A big part of why people will pay to hear you present is that they get great benefit from what you know. The other part is that they are not spending as much time learning as you.

Your job is to look, listen and learn.

a. *Look* – Look at what other successful
people are doing in this space and
model them. You should always be on
the lookout for something new to
learn.

b. *Listen* – Listen to the masters and what
they can teach you. Drop the ego.
There is a reason that they are already
the masters. Listen to what others are
saying. You can still draw your own
conclusions about the information,
but you do need to listen.

c. *Learn* – Learn from every experience. If
you fall flat on your face during a
presentation, don't say "I am just no
good at presenting." Instead, pick
yourself up and ask, "What can I learn
and apply from this experience?" By
focusing on what you can learn
instead of what you didn't do right,
you will enhance your skills for the
next presentation and the next. Strive

to learn something new every day.

6. **Plagiarize nicely.** You should not feel the need to put everything that another person said on your slide. When you are quoting someone, quote them. When you are building your presentation, don't put the whole thing into your PowerPoint. If you do this, you will be performing "death by bullet point" on your audience. Newsflash: lots of people now know <u>how</u> to read. You should not read your presentation, you should deliver it! So, put only what is necessary on the slide and the rest should come from you, not the projector.

7. **Before the Curtain Goes Up.** It is somewhat unrealistic to think that you will always be perfect. You will not be in presentation mode 24/7. If you are, you are likely to annoy people. The greatest presenters in the world still have a way of gearing up for the stage. We have broken that process down into three steps...

a. <u>The activation</u> – Each person will have
their own unique way of doing this.
Some people will let out a yell (not
advised in a big room). Others will
visualize success. Whatever anchor
you have come up with, use it. It
works! That activating anchor helps
you to change the pattern of your
brain waves. It is like an athlete going
through the perfect shot, the perfect
pass, the perfect punch or kick, before
they take action. My activation is four
slow deep breaths, and then the
clearing of my mind. I remove
anything but this present moment.

b. <u>The inspiration</u> – Each person will need
to allow their inspiration to flow from
them. We can only do this when we
are able to see the success that we are
bringing. In my mind, I construct my
audience around me. I see them
hanging on every word. I see them

applauding when they should, laughing at my jokes, and loving everything that I have to offer them. My body begins to vibrate with energy and I am ready for step three.

c. <u>THE UNLEASHING</u> – Imagine that you are a caged tiger, or whatever predatory animal you relate to, and that you are so ready to pounce on the subject that you are clawing at the cage walls. You simply need to be unleashed on the subject and the audience will be in absolute awe of what you have to offer. That "unleashing" is what puts you in full "state" and ready to give a killer presentation.

8. **May I have another helping, please?** You want them to want you back. You want them to go out of their way to find a way to bring you back on the same subject or on a new one. When you get them asking you to come

back, you will make your career secure. There are three easy steps to remember in order to make this happen.

  a. *Knock their socks off!* Nothing gets you invited back quite like actually being awesome! You need to deliver your best every single time you get up on stage. If your goal is to leave them pining for more because of how much fun they had and how much they learned, you are positioned for success.

  b. *Plant the seeds of your return.* You should have three to five points sprinkled throughout your presentation referencing other things, or more in-depth things that you can share with them if you come back. You begin with "if" in the first two points and switch to "when" in points three through five. This sets them to thinking about getting you back as soon as they can to get the rest of the valuable information that you have to offer.

c. *Drop the science.* The last point here is one that made other speakers pop themselves on the forehead after I gave it to them. One of the keys to my success has been to ask. Shocker! Right? I end my presentations by asking them to tell others about me and what they have learned. I tell them that it is alright to post about me on Facebook, Twitter and all other social media platforms. I let them know I am even okay with them buying a billboard to tell others how much they liked it. Then I make them laugh by saying "If you didn't like it, remember what my kindergarten teacher taught me: nobody likes a whiner." I usually get quite a bit of laughter on that one, but it works. They tell people. I get referrals. They are even happy to do it because I brought them value and I gave them permission to tell others.

So, we will leave you with this…

If you learned something from this book, if you got even one nugget of value, tell somebody! Tell them that the book was great! In fact, tell everyone on Amazon.com that the book was good by giving us a 5-star rating and sharing some of those warm fuzzy thoughts with the world. Quote the book and post links to it. If you want, you can order 1,000 copies for all of your social media friends. That seems a little excessive, but we are okay with it. Give the gift of removing boredom from presentations by buying copies of the book for your team. Do what you feel will make the world a better place. And, if you didn't like it, remember what our kindergarten teacher taught us, "nobody likes a whiner."

Now, go out and deliver the best presentations possible!

Jody Holland &
Mike Grigsby

ABOUT THE AUTHORS

Jody Holland is an author, speaker, and entrepreneur. He has started three successful companies, written thousands of pages of training, and published five books. He has spoken and presented in multiple countries and all across the United States. Jody's fun and witty style of "edu-tainment" engages audiences, entertains them, and educates them as well. His objective has always been to leave the minds of his audience in better shape than he found them. You can look for other books by Holland on Amazon.com.

Mike Grigsby as had an incredible and eclectic career in developing the best in others. Mike is an author, trainer, artist, graphic designer, and IT Manager. Mike has delivered thousands of training programs over his career, hundreds of keynote speeches, and has coached entrepreneurs and business leaders to incredible heights of creativity. Mike has always had a way of distilling information into its most entertaining format while keeping an audience on the edge of their seats.

Other Books By Jody Holland
All Books Can Be Purchased on
Amazon.com

Leadership Evo
*A practical guide for transforming leadership in your
organization and unlocking your highest potential!
**Has an accompanying 2-day program.
**Check out www.LeadershipEvo.com*

The Quest
Discovering God's purpose for you

Living The Quest
Putting the 8 lessons to work to live your quest

25 Activities In A Bag
Portable team-building programs

The 12 Principles of Success
12 principles to guide you to a more successful life.

Success: A 12-Step Program
*The 12 things that successful people consistently do.
Has an accompanying 2-day program*

Breakthrough Leadership
Living the TEAM CHIP model

Just Make Time
Managing what you allow into your time

Made in the USA
Middletown, DE
14 October 2021